GW00362509

Let God's Will
Find You

BOB YANDIAN

Let God's Will Find You
Copyright © 2016 by Bob Yandian Ministries

Bob Yandian Ministries
PO Box 55236
Tulsa, OK 74155
www.bobyandian.com

Table of Contents

Foreword

David, after he had served his own generation by the will of God, fell asleep.

(Acts 13:36)

The writer of Acts summed up a fulfilled life and peaceful death in one simple statement about David's life. *David served his own generation by the will of God.*

You have been left in this earth, after salvation, to serve your own generation. But it is impossible to successfully serve without knowing the unique will of God for you. You can do good works for the Lord as a Christian, work in your church, go on missions trips, and witness. But, no good works bring peace and fulfillment until you know you are producing them from the will, or call of God on your life.

I discovered the will of God for my life in my junior year at Oklahoma State University. The Lord spoke to me very clearly, and I began my quest to become a Bible teacher as soon as I left at the end of the semester. My call took me to Rhema Bible Training Center where I not only taught but became the dean of instructors. From there, I became the pastor of Grace Fellowship and led the congregation for 33 years before being led to return to instructing young ministers in Bible schools and minister conferences. I always thought the ministry would be a place of poverty, but was pleased to find financial prosperity was part of God's will for the Christian life. Yet, I came to a major conclusion, I would rather be poor and in God's will than rich and out of His will. There is no peace like being in the middle of God's will.

Although no Bible character, Old Testament or New, found the will of God for his life immediately, no one successfully served God without discovering God's call eventually. Our usual answer to those seeking God's will for their lives is to pray, and they will discover their call one day. Although prayer is good, this answer is simplistic and leaves many believers in frustration after years of seeming silence from heaven. God's method is not hidden, but open for all to see. One common thread unites all Bible believers together when it comes to finding God's will. This is why I wrote this book. I want to make the seemingly complicated simple.

Bro. Bob Yandian

Introduction

Major reason for discovering the will of God for a Christian is it answers the question of "why am I here?" We often think the sinner, the unbeliever, is the only one occupied with this question. But it continues to bother a Christian who wonders why God leaves us on earth after we join His family. In other words, becoming a Christian is not the only reason God placed us on the earth. The new birth is not the fulfillment of God's will for our life but the beginning. The new birth is the same for everyone who receives Jesus, but God's will for our life is as individual as each of us. Even though you might have the same call on your life as I do, how and where you are to fulfill it is personal and unique to you.

Not knowing God's will for your life can leave you in a wilderness of confusion. It is not as bad as the unbeliever, since we know we have found eternal life and a permanent home in heaven, but it can still be perplexing. How do you know when you have found His will? Or when it seems you have found it, is this really God's will or just your personal desire? Does a voice come from heaven? Does God still speak today through signs and wonders, visions and prophecies?

Personal Insight

I have found that when I discover the will of God, in any area of my life, it is like, somehow, I have always known it. I just did not understand until now. The events of my life and the fragments of His guidance now make sense. This is what God was leading me toward for years. And, just as the fragments of His guidance are like pieces of a puzzle that now form a more complete picture, so is His calling in life. My call is a piece of a puzzle for God's will in this world in this time period. I want this to be your revelation and response also as you read through this book.

How God's guidance is revealed to us is the subject of this book. It is not a cloudy or complicated subject in the Bible. It is very clear. We have just let personal opinions and the counsel of others cover up the simplicity of discovering God's will for our life.

ONE

The Making of a Successful Church

My father pastored three churches from the time I was five years old until I was in junior high school. The churches were located in small towns around Tulsa, where our family lived. The churches were also small in congregation numbers and controlled by small boards who seemed to have two goals in mind. Those goals were first to make the pastor do all the work of the ministry and second to pay him as little as possible to keep expenses low. My father had to balance visiting people in hospitals, homes, and prisons and doing weddings and funerals while also maintaining a job at American Airlines to keep the family from starving and losing our home.

He thought the next two churches would be better, but the same thinking seemed to be there also. No church members wanted to help because their reasoning was, if we hired him and paid him money, he should be doing the work.

He finally left pastoring and took our family to a large interdenominational church in Tulsa so he and my mother could find friends and my sister and I could find youth to fellowship with. It was here we discovered a great strength of a local church—people helping people. Many people were involved in teaching classes, caring for the children and youth, and visiting the sick in hospitals and homes. All believers are commanded to "let us do good to all, especially to those who are of the household of faith." (Galatians 6:10). It is from the faithful workers in the service that the pastor found new board members and staff to operate the church throughout the week. The pastor personally met with those he saw faithful and asked them to accept more responsibility.

A Generation Later

Our family later left that church to help begin another church. It took off rapidly and within a few years, became the largest church in the city of Tulsa. This pastor also built the church on faithful workers. Growth and maturity marked the people who attended. My wife, Loretta, and I helped in the children's ministry. I also worked the sound system and made recordings of the service for members of the congregation to purchase.

But, sadly, the church we had left went through many struggles with their pastor. He was older and after many years retired, leaving a vacancy in the pulpit. The board was faced with the responsibility of providing for him as well as finding a replacement. The former worship leader was contacted who had been gone from the church for years. He had been popular with the people and loved for his preaching ability as well as leading worship. After much prayer, he accepted the position and returned to Tulsa.

Upon returning to the once popular and well attended church, he found the church board and auditorium filled with the same older people he knew from years before. They bragged to him about how the church and the property and homes around the church used to house missionaries coming to the city were all owned and paid for. There was also a great surplus of money in the bank account. This might be a dream come true for any incoming pastor. But, the problems outweighed the blessings. There were no greeters, ushers, children or youth workers, or choir. He knew his first priority was to get the people working and helping to bring in a new and younger congregation. This was easier said than done.

He began a month long teaching on getting involved in the church. He taught on the benefits and fulfillment of people helping people in order to win them to Jesus and help fill the church. The first week he taught on becoming a greeter or usher. He asked for volunteers, and no one accepted. He taught the second week on teaching the children and youth, and again, when asked, no one volunteered. The third week he taught on becoming an outreach minister to visit the sick in homes and the hospital. And, again, no one volunteered. Finally he asked for those to sing in the choir and help usher people into the presence of God before the message was taught. You guessed it; no one volunteered.

But he noticed something interesting after he taught each week. The offerings went up when he asked for the people to assist and volunteer. This was confusing. So he went to the church board, those he had also known for years, and asked them why the money increased after he asked the people to become involved. They responded, "we expect you to hire them".

He told me the story over lunch one day and added some great insight. He said his dream would have always been to have a church paid for with money in the bank. But he now realized a great church cannot be measured with money. A successful church is people helping people.

Why Does God Want You To Be A Church Volunteer?

I pastored for 33 years and saw many people leave the church for full-time ministry. I have never found the exact number of church members who entered the ministry becoming missionaries, evangelists, teachers, worship leaders, pastors, and associates. But, they all had one thing in common. They were faithful volunteers in the church. Many never became full-time employees of the church, but God promoted them into other churches and ministries in our own country and around the world. Many of them I hated to lose. It seemed that after years of faithful service, they finally reached the level of trust and responsibility I had prayed for. At that time, many approached me and told me they felt a call into full time ministry and would be leaving the church. I laid hands on each one of them in front of the congregation and watched them ride off into the sunset.

I often complained to God while praying for them that I did not appreciate Him calling my best into the ministry, especially after years of preparation in the church. Why not let me get some satisfaction from their ministry now that they reached a place to be a great help? In fact, I told the Lord, there were many in the congregation I would gladly give Him if He would call them away. They were troublemakers and unwilling to work. I had prayed they would leave, but they were still there. The Lord spoke to me one time while I was complaining and said, "which one would you rather have, a one hundred fold return on the faithful one or the problem one?" So, I sowed the good ones and saw God bring even better ones into the church.

Volunteering is helpful for the church, but it also helps you, the volunteer. Throughout the Bible, especially in the New Testament church, faithful volunteers were promoted into greater positions in the ministry. Paul told us in 1 Timothy 3:13 that "a deacon who is found to be faithful purchases to himself promotion and great boldness."

Out of the seven young men chosen in Acts 6 to help serve the needs of the widows, the first two chosen, Stephen and Phillip, went into full time ministry and were the subjects of the next two chapters. Because they were faithful over a few things, God made them rulers over much. In other words, whatever your hand finds to do, do it with all your might. People and leaders are watching. So is God.

Two

How Do You Find
A Marriage Partner?

The Lord God caused a deep sleep
to fall on Adam and he slept. And
He took one of his ribs and closed
up the flesh around it. And from the
rib, which the Lord God had taken
from the man, He made a woman and
brought her to the man.

(Genesis 2:21, 22)

Another question that is often asked is
"How do I find God's mate for me?"
Stories abound from couples of how they
came together and the circumstances which
brought them to each other. Seminars on

marriage and dating are spread across the country and college and career classes in churches or home groups are very popular.

Adam and Eve are our example of God's plan to unite a young man and woman together. How long Adam waited for his bride we do not know. We do know Adam was created on the sixth day (Genesis 1:26, 27) and formed from the dust of the ground (Genesis 2:7). However, we do not know how many days passed before God made a woman for him. God had a plan for the man to fulfill before his helper was brought to him.

What Had Adam Been Doing?

Let's go back a few verses and see what God instructed Adam to do before He made Eve.

> And The Lord God took the man, and placed him in the Garden of Eden to work it and guard it... And Adam gave names to all cattle, to the birds of the

air, and to every animal of the field;
but for Adam there was not found a
helper for him of his own species.

(Genesis 2:15, 20)

Adam was placed in a job before he was
given a woman. God's first command to Adam
was to be fruitful, multiply, and replenish the
earth (Genesis 1:28). This means God's first
promise to Adam was a wife. But before God
gave him a wife, He gave him a job.

Adam was to work in the garden and
name all the animals. God brought the animals to Adam, and whatever Adam called
them, that became their name. They had to
have been brought to Adam in pairs. As they
walked away, after being named, Adam must
have realized each animal came in twos. Yet,
he was only one. Every animal had a helper of
its own species, except for Adam. After Adam
named the animals, God made a woman for
him because he was alone. No other species
was alone. Notice, Adam was not lonely,

but alone. He had no capacity to be lonely in a perfect garden with a perfect God. But he needed a mate for companionship and to fulfill God's plan for multiplication and replenishing the earth.

Four Points on Finding a Mate

The story of Adam, from the day he was created until the day God made a woman for him can be explained in four points for us to observe. The first two points are for us to do, and the second two points are God's response to our obedience.

1. Get To Work: Adam was given a job before he was given a woman. In other words, Adam began to provide for a woman he did not have yet. Young women need to be warned not to become serious over a young man who doesn't have a job. They usually say, "we can live off of love." Grocery stores do not take love checks, and department stores do not take love credit cards. They only take money forms backed by cash. Also, young men need to be taught they need a job and begin to learn to provide for a woman they do not have yet. This is truly trust in God to provide a mate for one who has decided to act responsibly. Along with a secular job, get involved in church helping other Christians. In church is usually where you will meet your mate.

2. Go to Sleep: If you have truly put your trust in God to provide a mate, then you need to rest on God's word and His promises. You cannot provide for yourself. God will provide for you if you trust in Him and rest. Like Jesus rested on a pillow during the storm, so can you rest on each promise. There are over seven thousand promises in God's word. Each one is like a pillow for you to rest on, waiting for God to come through for you. For we who have believed do enter that rest (Hebrews 4:9).

3. God Will Provide a Mate for You: Just as He made a woman for Adam, God will provide a mate for you. When Adam woke out of his sleep, he saw someone who was beautiful and perfectly made for him. Will He do less for you?

4. God Will Bring the Person to You: This is important. You do not have to run from church to church and single's group to single's group. "Stand still and see the deliverance of the Lord" (Exodus 14:13) was the word of Moses to the children of Israel at the Red Sea. We often become guilty of trying to help God. God promises to bring us the right person. We get impatient and head for a dating website, even ones for Christians. What did God do before the computer was invented? Computers match us to a person as close to us as possible, sharing the same likes and dislikes. Most married couples I know, including me and my wife, are opposites in most of our likes. I like action movies, she likes love stories. She likes classical music, and I like classic rock. I am a day person; she is a night person. Let God provide a mate and bring them to you. Quit telling God what you want and realize God knows you better than you do.

Bible Examples

Isaac wanted a wife but stayed at his home, minding the fields while sending out a servant to find a mate. The servant found Rebecca and brought her back to Isaac. The moment she climbed off her camel, after a long ride, their eyes met, and they knew they were right for each other. You too have a servant, the Holy Spirit, you may send out to find a partner for your life.

Jacob was working with Laban's sheep when he met Rachel. He was not searching for a life partner, but God provided. He also fell in love with her shortly after they met.

The love story of Boaz and Ruth greatly amplify these four points. Ruth's husband had died in Moab and she accompanied her mother-in-law to Israel in faith. Not looking for a husband, she took a job gleaning in the fields and happened to end up working in a rich man's field, Boaz. Boaz saw her working in the field and something stirred in him. He inquired of her and arranged to meet her. They fell in love, married, and became the great grandparents of David the king. They also became part of the lineage of Israel's Messiah, Jesus (Matthew 1:5-16).

Start Them Young

I taught this passage in church one Sunday on the importance of a young man having a job before meeting the girl he wants to date. A teenage boy came to me after church and took the sermon seriously. He told me he was still living at home with his parents and had no expenses. The only thing he was saving his money for was a car. He told me he was going to take a second job and begin saving money for the girl God would bring to him to date and eventually marry. He met a young girl in church a year later, and they dated for a year. At the end of that year, he proposed, and gave her a ring he bought with cash. One year after they were engaged, they were married. He then placed a down payment on a home for them to live in. He skipped the whole entry level apartment or trailer park and went directly to living in a home. The Tulsa newspaper ran an article on him many years later as one of the most prosperous businessmen in the city. I like to think I had a part to play in his success when I taught these scriptures that Sunday.

This Is How I Met My Wife

Loretta and I met in the church choir while I was attending Oklahoma State University. I came home every weekend because I loved church and wanted to remain in contact with my Christian friends. One week, my sister called me and told me my future wife had joined the church and the choir. I told her to mind her own business, but when I met Loretta, I knew it too. We have both heard the Lord speak to us and direct our life and calling. God has truly made us one and I could not have found a better wife on my own or from a web site if it had existed.

All the Way from Arkansas

A young girl who attended the church I pastored in Tulsa told my wife and me one day she was leaving the church. She was one of the best praise and worship leaders we had, and we hated to lose her. When I asked her why, she said she had been looking and all the good young men in the church were taken and the only ones left were old or previously married. She was going to another church to look for a young man to date. I told her this story of Adam and Eve coming together at the right time and told her to wait. She should get more involved in the church, and my wife and I would agree with her in prayer for a young man to come. She was reluctant but, after our prayer, did as I asked and became more involved in the church worship team than ever.

In a city in northwest Arkansas, a young home builder heard the voice of the Holy Spirit telling him to move to Tulsa. No more direction was given, and he fought the moving of God for a month before finally saying "yes." He moved to Tulsa, and his home building business took off rapidly. Within weeks, he was busier than ever, yet still wondering why the Lord had directed him to move to this city. As he was driving one morning to frame a new home, the Holy Spirit told him to attend the church he was driving past. It was the church I pastored. The following Sunday, he attended and ended up sitting on the aisle, across from the girl we had agreed with in prayer. It was not her Sunday to lead worship, but to sit in the church service. The two caught each other out of the corner of their eyes and ended up exchanging phone numbers after church. They dated for a quite a while and were married. They later ended up in the Philippines as missionaries. She got to work in the church and rested on God's promise to provide a husband. God then found someone just for her and delivered him to the church and to the seat right across from her. Do you think God would do that for you? I think so. You stand in a long line of successes found in God's word and in everyday life.

What Does This Have To Do With Finding God's Will For My Life?

You are probably asking yourself this question after two chapters dealing with everything but finding God's will for your life. What does working in a church and helping God's people have to do with finding His will? Also, you might already have a husband or wife and thought this chapter was useless for your life. You might be tempted to put this book down at this point, thinking I have missed the whole point of the subject of this book. How am I to find the will of God for my life? Well, go with me to the next chapter.

THREE

The Template of God's Plan for You

I'll give you four points for discovering the will of God for your life. The first two are for you to do, and the second two are for God. First, get to work. Second, go to sleep. Third, God will create a perfect plan for your life. And, fourth, God will bring His plan to you. You can plainly see it is no different for finding God's will in life than it is to find a mate. Actually, this plan, this template, is the same for almost every plan God has for you while you are on earth.

First, Get a Job

This is not specifically a secular job, but one helping God's people. Most of the time this will have to do with helping believers in the local church, ushering, greeting, counseling, singing in praise and worship, or helping children or youth. Galatians tells us "to do good to all men, but especially those of the household of faith" (Galatians 6:10). Your ministry to God's people will help train you for ministering to the world. When God finds you, He wants to see you helping with His kingdom. It is just like those who found a marriage partner in the word of God. I can find no place in scripture where God brought His will to those who were praying or sitting waiting. Moses was watching over Jethro's sheep when he came across the burning bush. David was also watching sheep when Samuel came to his father's house to anoint the next king of Israel. Gideon was on the threshing floor and Elisha was plowing a field when approached with their call in life.

The disciples were fishing and collecting taxes when Jesus found and called them.

Don't get me wrong, prayer is important in finding the will of God, but it is not the most important thing. It is an important step on the path to the answer. Prayer makes you sensitive to God's will so when He does bring His plan to you, you will recognize Him. Let me add one important point to the issue of prayer. To make the most of your prayers for God's will, or any part of God's plan for that matter, be praying in the Holy Spirit, praying in other tongues. This makes you more sensitive to the voice of the Holy Spirit (1 Corinthians 14:4) and less distracted by the voices of the world. I have a pair of noise reducing headphones for my trips on airplanes. They help lower the outside sounds so I can hear the music or teaching lessons more clearly. Praying in tongues is God's set of noise reducing headphones. It does not amplify the voice of the will of God, but it does reduce the noise of the world so you can hear God's voice better. The still small voice does not change.

Second, Go To Sleep

It will do you no good to stay up late at night worrying about your calling or fretting because God has not come through for you during your time frame. You often think you are waiting on God, when He may be waiting on you to start working and quit worrying and complaining. God promised in His word He would come through for you. So, rest on His promises. Come to the point where you don't care how long it takes. You will just keep being a blessing to other people for the rest of your life if that is what is necessary. Your greatest fulfillment does not come from finding God's will for your life, but from being a blessing and a help to other people. This lets you sleep like a baby at night. At the right time, God's plan will find you if you don't give up. In other words, in due season, you will reap if you don't faint.

Third, God Will Create a Perfect Plan for Your Life

You are unique, and so is God's plan for you. I am a pastor and teacher, like many millions of believers around the world, but my ministry style and presentation is unique to me. This is God's gift working in my life. God does not have a boiler plate call to a ministry but one tailor made to you. While you are working and resting on His promises, God is making a plan for your life and personality like no one else's. Eve was perfectly made for Adam. God took a common rib and made a unique woman. God will begin with a common call and make a unique plan out of it just for you. Adam did not know God was creating a woman for him. He was resting. God woke him up to show him what He had been working on for a long time.

Fourth, God Will Bring His Will to You

You do not have to run from ministry conference to ministry conference. You do not have to seek a prophet or one who operates in a word of knowledge. Those people are truly ministers of God, but they are not the Holy Spirit in your life. God is not hiding His will. He is still working on it. Once He finishes and finds you working and resting, He will bring it to you. You will wake up on day and discover a plan custom made for you.

A Bible School Diploma Is Not Enough

Tulsa is filled with Bible and ministry school graduates who are still attending churches in the area years after their graduation. They will not help in church or become involved, because they are waiting on God to bring His call to their lives. Any moment, the heavens will open, and they will end up with a ministry bigger than anyone else's in the country.

A young ministry school graduate in our church caught my attention when I found out he was excellent with a camera. I needed a church photographer and asked him if he would take pictures of the church events for me to place in our monthly publication. He would only need to show up, take a few pictures, and leave. I would gladly pay him for the shots he took. I was surprised when he said, "no." He told me he was called to the mission field and expected the door to open within a few weeks. He did not want to commit then have to find someone else to fulfill the job. I agreed to look for someone else, but week after week, I saw him in church. I asked him a second time and received a more emphatic "no." He felt the call was going to manifest within days. A month later, I told him I had found no one. He again told me the door was about to open, he felt it in his heart, and would not commit. I told him I did not believe the door would open until he helped in the church. His faithfulness over a small job would show God he was capable of handling much more. He decided to help and took pictures in our church for three years. When the door to Eastern Europe opened, he was a much more settled and fulfilled Christian, ready to work for God wherever he was placed. After many years, our church still supports him and his family in the Middle East.

True happiness in the Christian life is found by waiting on God and His perfect will for you. God will find you. He knows exactly where you are and wants to find you doing something, working when He does. "Blessed is that servant, whom his Lord when he comes will find him so doing" (Luke 12:43).

Quit coveting other people's call or dictating to God what you should have. You are not other people and comparing yourself to them is useless (2 Corinthians 10:12). He broke the mold when He made other ministers and He did the same when He created you in His Son, Jesus Christ. So, your call will be like no one else's, and you will affect the world like no one else. Father truly does know best.

Meet Bob Yandian

Bob Yandian was the pastor of Grace Church in his hometown of Tulsa, Oklahoma for 33 years. In 2013 he began a new phase of ministry and passed the baton to his son, Robb, who now pastors Grace Church. Bob now travels extensively, training up a new generation in the word of God at Bible schools, minister conferences, and churches.

Bob attended Southwestern College and is also a graduate of Trinity Bible College. He has served as both instructor and dean of instructors at Rhema Bible Training Center. He also established the School of the Local Church/Grace School of Ministry that has raised up and sent out hundreds of ministers to churches and missions organizations around the world. He is called "a pastor to pastors."

Contact Information

Bob Yandian Ministries
PO Box 55236
Tulsa, OK 74155

Phone: 800.284.0595
Email: bym@bobyandian.com
Web: www.bobyandian.com